Celestial

Umama Suriya

Celestial © 2023 Umama Suriya

All rights reserved.

No part of this publication may be reproduced, stored in a retrieval system, or transmitted, in any form or by any means, electronic, mechanical, photocopying, recording or otherwise, without the prior written permission of the presenters.

Umama Suriya asserts the moral right to be identified as author of this work.

Presentation by *BookLeaf Publishing*

Web: www.bookleafpub.com

E-mail: info@bookleafpub.com

ISBN: 9789357744225

First edition 2023

To my younger self. She never thought the day she could hold her published book in her hands would come. Yet that day is here.

To my parents, my two brothers Gilman Suriya and Yaman Suriya, my cousin and twin sister Amna Adnan Suriya, and every single person that has had a positive impact on my life and my writing.

ACKNOWLEDGEMENT

Thank you to my best friend since middle school, Rakeb Temam, for helping me with the order and editing of these poems and for always being a cheerleader for my dreams. Thank you to Samahir Abdulkadir for being an older sister to me, and also taking pictures of me for my author headshot, slowly helping me gain confidence in everything I do. Some other people I truly appreciate and have been there for me are Yash Ravula, Tabitha Tudor, Dana Farsakh, Yasmeen Farsakh, Manasi Vipat, Nawal Seif, Nila Jeyapriya, Jessica Reyna, Yusra Ibrahim, Ashtyn Hurst, Ammar Mahuwala, Haroon Abdulkadir, Hussein Abdel Aziz, and others that have been with me in my journey of growing as a person and a writer.

your life.

your life is like a rose,
 it blooms during the spring and stays bloomed.
 but as winter comes around, they start to go,
leaving behind
 dead petals on the fertile soil,
 and a place where they'll grow back and come
again.

 your life is like a tree,
 with its leaves on its branches.
 until autumn comes, and
 the leaves fall from the trees, leaving the tree
bare,
 and a place where they'll grow back and come
again.

 your life is like the grass,
 the scorching sun shining on top of it,
 making the grass dry, turning a yellow color.
 the color of green goes away from the grass, but
there's still hope,
 and a place where they'll grow back and come
again.

 no matter what you're going through,

it'll all pass eventually.
nature experiences change too, but they all
adapt; it's the circle of life.
it's yours too, so be happy,
and know that you'll have a place where you'll
grow back to normal
and thrive again to show who you truly are to
the universe.

your space matters.

there's a distinct difference
between a good person
and one that tries to be one
one's universe seems to be aligned
to help them succeed
and one's universe is slowly shifting
but in reality,
what makes a good person good?
and why does the universe
treat actually good people
like unwanted space matter?

paradise.

the cold light blue water
 approaching up to your toes as
 the earth pushes up against your feet.
 the hard little rocks and soft sand
 getting stuck in between your toes
 as you close your eyes and feel the wind in your
hair.
 the waves crashing, you feel paradise.

fantasy of you.

why is it that
every single time i want you
the fantasy of you shows up
never physically you

how long do i have to wait
for you to realize
that you love me the same
as you do in my daydreams.

the way you look at me.

i can't help but smile
every time you look at me
or respond to a comment i said
you stare right at me while talking
the prolonged eye contact
as if you know i am a person of comfort
when your nerves take you away
from being able to speak your truth
it's like we know
we are a person of comfort to each other
in a stormy, anxiety-filled world.

you're in my imagination.

i take your hand in mine
and lead you into my mind
where rainbows were replaced
by an overarching shadow
and butterflies lost their wings,
stuck feeding on one dying flower.

it's alright, you can see me like this
but don't you worry
because i know your imagination mirrors mine
don't feed off of my gloom
adding on to your gloomy little world
that you worked so hard to hide.

i finally take you in
and see myself smile
you gave the butterflies their wings back
so i squeezed your hand and thanked you
for shifting my reality
from gloom to pure ecstasy.

let me into your imagination
where gloom can be replaced with love
and the broken glass on the floor
can be miraculously fixed

let me bandage the wound on your wrist
and help you heal to your best self.

come into my imagination, anytime
where you always existed
hidden away under billions of tears
replaced by your contagious smile
finally, rainbows appear again
and butterflies flutter away to new flowers.

sunshine.

9

you were sunshine in human form
 and i was the clouds that covered your rays
 i covered you for too long
 somehow blinding myself in the process

 not letting you shine for others
 i realized other people needed your sunshine
 for most people have experienced lightning
 and have a desire for sunshine to come and fix
everything.

moon.

you stare at the moon's light aimlessly every day
 waiting for the day it would be complete
 mourning its loss the next day
 yet excited for its new beginning

 your optimism of its return
 could shadow everybody's grief of the moon's
disappearance
 convincing me to be optimistic
 when you, my moon, disappears.

 you made me realize,
 that i should be sure you'll return.

shooting star.

i was delighted to know the joyful magic
your smile could enlighten in others
it was quite easy to be enchanted
by your impeccable charm
reminding one of the brightest star
that turned itself into a shooting star overnight.

dove.

what happens when
a dove flies too close to the sun
do its wings burn and turn into ash
or does its purity dignify the burning nature
of the sun's usual fire

do doves know they're perfect
or do the clouds fail to proclaim that thought
underestimating the dove's intentions
to bestow perfection on all the lands
but the dove's wing —

it had burned and turned into ash.

i want you back.

there are times
things happen
and i want to scream out your name
and tell you every detail
but then i realize i can't
because you no longer exist
in the same universe as me
you're gone and i can't do anything
but patiently wait
for when you'll hop out of your own world
and join me in mine
but if you do leave your land because of me
would i be considered selfish?

i watch you grow.

you think i'm lying when i say that i love you
everything i do, i think about you
i think of peace when i think of you
you know you're no good alone
why do you try to be better than everyone
when you know you're breaking down
it's okay to be falling into an abyss
feeling like you're nowhere
you're in my arms
take me in
remember me
when your seeds grow into trees
remember i was the one who planted you
keep that in mind as you look at the sunsets
watching the colors i'm painting for you
remember me.

the way he moved.

15

there was something so admirable
in the way he moved forward
waiting for change
but internally he knew
the world would always fail him.

these words were never mine.

these words were never mine to write
 yet i'm here writing them
 for i have found myself to be the victim
 in a situation that i should've listened
 i should've held your hands
 and realized the path i was taking you to
 blinded, i couldn't see where we were going
 for my focus was if i held your hand tight
enough
 instead of hearing you tell me that it hurt
 i led us into a never ending black hole.

i was vile, you were evil.

under the same beautiful moon as i
was you
the one that reminded me
that my flaws still exist
and the mistakes i've made
still linger in people's hearts
eating away at their insecurities
until they overwhelm them
and they think of my face
and remember wicked words
tear rolling down their eyes
wishing i would disappear
and at the same time
wishing i could exist
to be the epitome of vile
despite my angel eyes
and my deep white smile
and that one time
being the only time
i ever felt like maybe
i am capable
of being vile
to only those that were
malevolent to me first.

hope.

why is it that,
 the races you run,
 the miles of pain you chase away from,
 how come everyone always tells you to have
hope?

why is it that,
 every heartbreak,
 every single negativity told about you,
 is lost when hope gets in the picture?

why is it that,
 the nights you spent crying,
 the days you gave up,
 why did hope fix everything?

everything that happens in this world,
 it can be easily resolved.

let hope be on your side,
 and you'll win any battle you're fighting.

the sun is rising.

the sun is rising before my eyes
 i've made it another day
 the whispers of animals
 the chirps of birds
 as they wake for dawn
 and i stare at the sun's light
 after watching moon's surrounding darkness
 that i love so much
 and realize i've made it another day.
 i've seen the light
 i can't help but smile
 i didn't let myself wither
 until darkness is all i could see
 i let myself live another day
 to see the light and hear the birds talk
 and damn, i can't help but say
 i'm proud of myself.

our roses bloomed.

we were like a black and white film
bland, but we always imagined color together
with every picture of the sequence
in order, we recreated our story
colorless, but we bloomed it with color
always painting the monotonous film with red
roses were our favorite view.

we were like a film camera
with every roll of film we use up
we imagined the pictures we took
the patience of waiting for development
some blurry, but we didn't care
there were roses behind every perfect photo.

we were like the human eye
the perfect sight, yet so unfortunate at times
we learned how to go back to normal
despite not knowing what that meant
we were bruised, the sunlight blinded us
but we were okay - our roses still bloomed.

forecast.

21

i had never came across an everlasting rainbow
until i got involved with you
somehow, rain clouds turned into
sunlight.

your winds could create tornadoes
but with me,
your winds never turned
deadly.

happily ever after.

i used to think
happily ever after was impossible
suddenly, my perspective changed
when i laid eyes on you
i started to think happy ever afters
were like a planetary alignment
very rare yet astonishing
and when the stars aligned
and i got to know you
i found out
that my happily ever after
was there all along.

happily ever after
was the ever after
that was always intended
for us.

celestial.

everything that is celestial
 reminds me of my love for you
 for me,
 you are my earth, my sun, and my moon.

www.ingramcontent.com/pod-product-compliance
Lightning Source LLC
LaVergne TN
LVHW051249200726
843510LV00011B/1767